Northeast Temperate Network Water Quality Report, 2006-2009

Acadia National Park

Natural Resource Data Series NPS/NETN/NRDS—2010/125

William G. Gawley

National Park Service
Acadia National Park
PO Box 177
Bar Harbor, Maine 04609

December 2010
U.S. Department of the Interior
National Park Service
Natural Resource Program Center
Fort Collins, CO

The National Park Service, Natural Resource Program Center publishes a range of reports that address natural resource topics of interest and applicability to a broad audience in the National Park Service and others in natural resource management, including scientists, conservation and environmental constituencies, and the public.

The Natural Resource Data Series is intended for the timely release of basic data sets and data summaries. Care has been taken to assure accuracy of raw data values, but a thorough analysis and interpretation of the data has not been completed. Consequently, the initial analyses of data in this report are provisional and subject to change.

All manuscripts in the series receive the appropriate level of peer review to ensure that the information is scientifically credible, technically accurate, appropriately written for the intended audience, and designed and published in a professional manner.

This report received informal peer review by subject-matter experts who were not directly involved in the collection, analysis, or reporting of the data. Data in this report were collected and analyzed using methods based on established, peer-reviewed protocols and were analyzed and interpreted within the guidelines of the protocols.

Views, statements, findings, conclusions, recommendations, and data in this report do not necessarily reflect views and policies of the National Park Service, U.S. Department of the Interior. Mention of trade names or commercial products does not constitute endorsement or recommendation for use by the U.S. Government.

This report is available from the Northeast Temperate Network website (http://science.nature.nps.gov/im/units/NETN/Reports/reports.cfm) and the Natural Resource Publications Management website (http://www.nature.nps.gov/publications/NRPM).

Please cite this publication as:

Gawley, W. G. 2010. Northeast Temperate Network water quality report, 2006-2009: Acadia National Park. Natural Resource Data Series NPS/NETN/NRDS—2010/125. National Park Service, Fort Collins, Colorado.

NPS 123/106294, December 2010

Contents

Figures

Tables

Introduction

This is the first report on the water quality of Acadia National Park (ACAD) generated by the Northeast Temperate Network (NETN) Water Quality Monitoring Program. This report includes data gathered during the first four years of the monitoring program (2006-2009) and displays these results in graphic form, accompanied by a brief interpretation.

The vital signs for lakes, ponds and streams included in the NETN Freshwater Monitoring Protocol (Lombard et al. 2006) are water quality, nutrient enrichment, water quantity, and the detection of invasive plant species. These metrics were chosen to address the NPS Inventory and Monitoring objective to detect change in the status of physical, chemical, or biological attributes of the ecosystem.

The NETN freshwater monitoring protocol calls for a total of 37 park lakes and streams to be sampled monthly from May through October, with 11 sites monitored annually and the remainder visited on a two year (streams) or three year (lakes) rotating schedule. Park staff measure physical and in-situ water chemistry parameters each month, and periodically gather water samples for analysis at the University of Maine's (UMO) Sawyer Environmental Chemistry Research Laboratory. Additionally, stage height (water level) is recorded weekly at 17 lakes during the open-water season. All monitoring data are incorporated into a series of comprehensive databases that ultimately feed the U.S. Environmental Protection Agency's (EPA)"STORET" data system, the repository for all NPS water quality and quantity data.

Sampling Sites

The Acadia National Park lake and stream sites monitored by the NETN are mapped in Figure 1. Eight lake sites are sampled annually, while nine additional lakes are monitored as a part of a rotating design in which each lake is sampled every third year. Three continuous-record stream sites (with streamflow gages in which data are collected with automated dataloggers) are sampled annually, and seventeen partial-record stream sites (monthly streamflow data collection) are sampled using a rotating design where each site is sampled every other year. A maximum of nine partial-record sites and three continuous-record stream sites are sampled each year.

Methods

Monthly sampling parameters include basic water quality measures (pH, specific conductance, temperature, and dissolved oxygen) determined with a YSI 600XL water quality sonde as shown in Figure 2, as well as Secchi transparency (lakes), weather, stream flow (discharge), and stage. In May (streams only), June (lakes only) and August (lakes and streams), in addition to in-situ water chemistry, water samples are obtained and analyzed for acid neutralizing capacity (ANC), color, and nutrients. In the lakes, the water sample is a depth-integrated epilimnetic sample, and chlorophyll *a* is analyzed in addition to the other parameters.

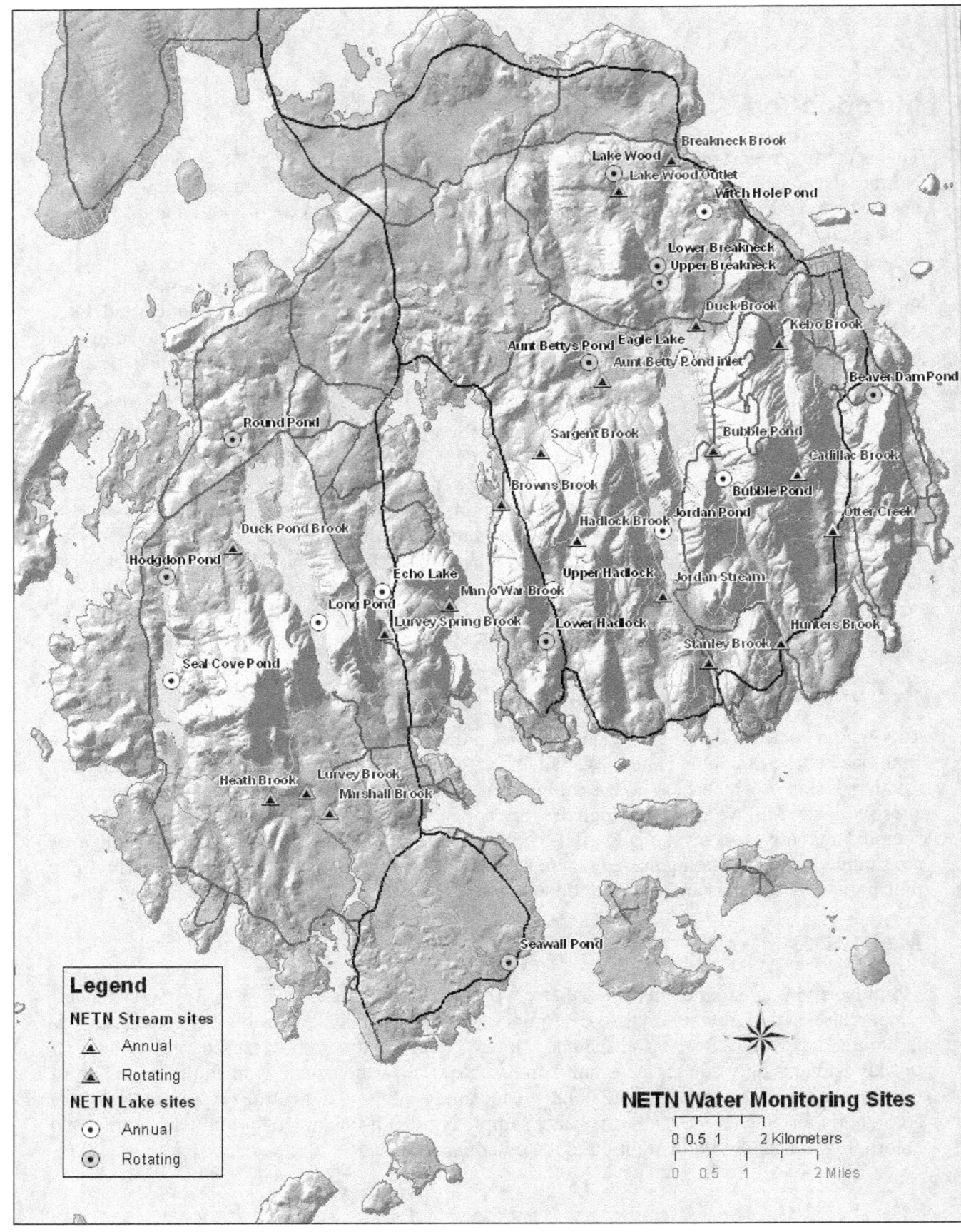

Figure 1. Acadia National Park freshwater monitoring sites.

The lake sampling procedure entails collecting all in-situ measurements and water samples from the deep hole (or center, in the case of lakes with uniform bathymetry) of the lake. Nutrient chemistry parameters are analyzed from a series of epilimnion core samples (4-10 meter depth) integrated in a churn splitter if the lake is stratified, or a half-meter grab sample if the lake is unstratified.

Stream discharge is measured at the partial record sites using U.S. Geological Survey (USGS) protocols, employing a measuring tape, wading rod, and Price pygmy current meter to measure a particular cross-sectional area of the stream and the velocity of the water at that cross section (Figure 3). Stream water quality measurements and water samples are collected in close proximity to the location of the discharge measurement. Sonde measurements are taken in the main stream flow, with care taken that the sonde is not resting directly on the stream bottom. Grab samples are taken by submerging the sample bottle directly in the stream with a gloved hand. A peristaltic pump and Tygon tubing are used to collect samples if water levels are too low to completely submerge a bottle.

A USGS permanent record gaging station was established at Otter Creek in May 2006, funded by the NETN. This site serves as an index gage for all the streams in the park by providing detailed streamflow information about one stream, allowing for estimates of loads of constituents at this site, and providing data to make estimates of streamflow at hydrologically similar ungaged sites or partial-record sites. Global Water WL-16 level loggers were installed at the Hadlock and Cadillac Brook sites to provide seasonal continuous water level data (though not accessible in "real-time") at two former USGS sites.

Figure 2. Beth Arsenault takes a lakewater chemistry profile with the YSI multiparameter sonde. *(Photo by M. Goff)*

Figure 3. Meghan Goff obtains a discharge (streamflow) measurement with a Price pygmy current meter. *(Photo by B. Arsenault)*

EPA Nutrient Criteria

Since Maine has no numeric water quality standards to which Acadia National Park monitoring data can be compared, EPA Ecoregion 8 water quality criteria (U.S. Environmental Protection Agency, 2002) are used as a benchmark in this report (Table 1). EPA water quality criteria for nutrients help translate narrative criteria within State or Tribal water quality standards by establishing values for causal variables (e.g., total nitrogen and total phosphorus) and response variables (e.g., turbidity and chlorophyll *a*). Causal variables are necessary to provide sufficient protection of designated uses before impairment occurs and to maintain downstream uses. Early response variables are necessary to provide warning signs of possible impairment and to integrate the effects of variable and potentially unmeasured nutrient loads.

Table 1. EPA Ecoregion 8 nutrient criteria.

Nutrient Criteria	Streams	Lakes
Total Phosphorus (ug/L)	10.00	8.00
Total Nitrogen (mg/L)	0.38	0.24
Chlorophyll *a* (ug/L)	0.63	2.43
Secchi disk depth (m)	N/A	4.93

These criteria were developed specifically for Ecoregion 8 (which includes the entire states of Maine, New Hampshire, and Vermont) and are designed to represent conditions of surface waters that are minimally impacted by human activities and thus protect against the adverse effects of nutrient enrichment from cultural eutrophication. The values are EPA's scientific recommendations regarding ambient concentrations of nutrients that protect aquatic resource quality. They do not hold any regulatory authority.

Climate

Both seasonal and annual shifts in precipitation and temperatures can have distinctive short-term and cumulative effects on stream flow, lake levels, physical lake properties, and water chemistry. Mean monitoring season (April through October) precipitation measured at the McFarland Hill National Atmospheric Deposition Program (NADP) site at Acadia National Park headquarters for the period 1982-2009 was 741.4 millimeters. Precipitation during the monitoring season from 2006 to 2009 was consistently above average, and air temperatures and solar radiation were typical of conditions recorded over the past decade. (Table 2, Figures 4 and 5).

Table 2. Average monitoring season (April-October) weather conditions

Year	Average Air Temp (C)	Average Solar Radiation (w/cm^2)	Average Monthly Precipitation (mm)	Total Precipitation (mm)
2006	13.9	193	163	1,140
2007	14.2	194	116	809
2008	13.4	191	118	826
2009	12.5	176	156	1,089

Mean Monthly Air Temperature and Solar Radiation (ACAD 2006-2009)

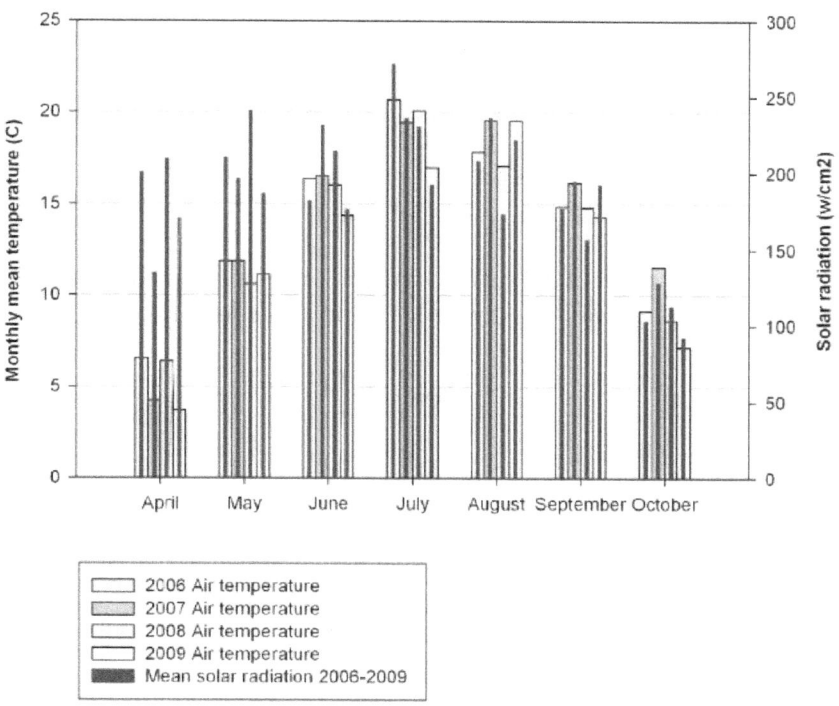

Figure 4. Temperature and solar radiation data from the Acadia National Park air quality monitoring site.

Mean Monthly Precipitation (ACAD 2006-2009)

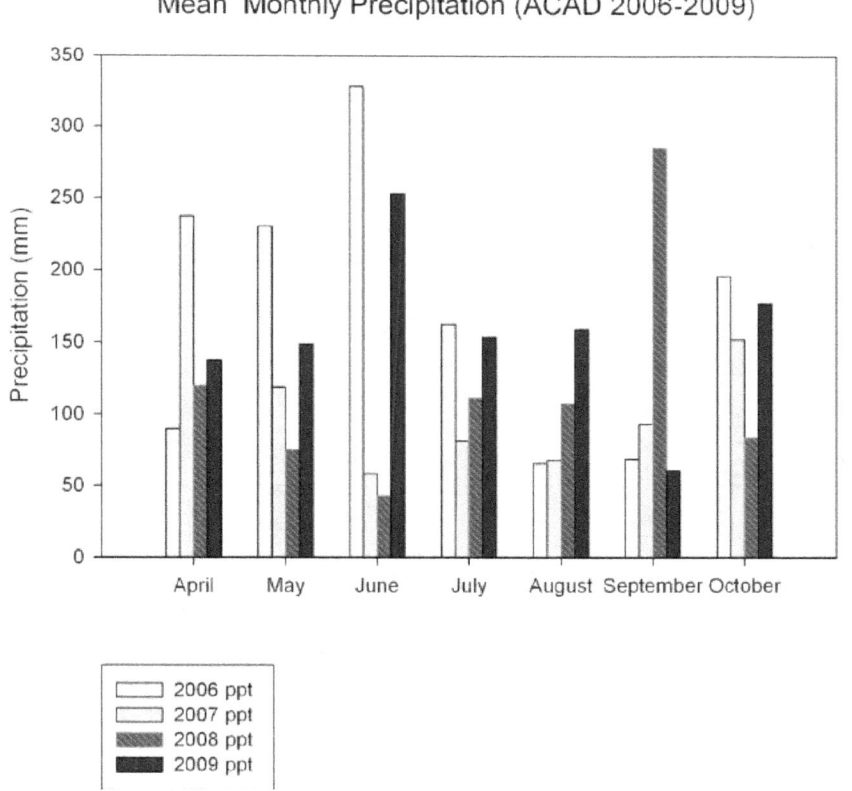

Figure 5. Precipitation data from the Acadia National Park air quality monitoring site.

Results

Monitoring results are displayed in time series graphs showing all data for each site for a given parameter. Most data gaps are by design, for example the planned pauses between sampling series (no samples collected during winter months) and rotating panels of sites. As data richness increases, trends may emerge from these time series graphs.

If EPA or other water quality criteria exist for a particular parameter they are displayed on the graphs. In addition, error bars are included whenever possible, representing $\pm$ 1 standard deviation.

Locations are labeled by NETN site codes. The lists of site codes for lakes and streams are in Table 3.

Table 3. NETN site codes for Acadia NP surface waters

Lake	NETN Code	Stream	NETN Code
Aunt Bettys	ACANTB	Aunt Bettys Pond inlet	ACABIN
The Bowl	ACBOWL	Breakneck Brook	ACBRKB
Bear Brook Pond	ACBRBK	Browns Brook	ACBRWN
Bubble Pond	ACBUBL	Bubble Pond Outlet	ACBUBO
Duck Pond	ACDKPD	Cadillac Stream	ACCADS
Eagle Lake	ACEAGL	Duck Pond Brook (inlet to Long Pond)	ACDKLI
Echo Lake	ACECHO	Duck Brook (Eagle Lake outlet)	ACEGLO
Hodgdon Pond	ACHODG	Hadlock Brook	ACHADB
Jordan Pond	ACJORD	Hunters Brook	ACHNTR
Lower Breakneck	ACLBRK	Heath Brook	ACHTHB
Lower Hadlock	ACLHAD	Jordan Stream (Jordan Pond outlet)	ACJRDO
Long Pond (MDI)	ACLONG	Kebo Brook	ACKEBO
Long Pond (IAH)	ACLPIH	Lake Wood Outlet	ACLKWO
Round Pond	ACROUN	Lurvey Spring Brook (Echo Lake inlet)	ACLSIE
Sargent Mtn Pond	ACSAMP	Lurvey Brook	ACLVYB
Seal Cove Pond	ACSEAL	Man o'War Brook	ACMOWB
Seawall Pond	ACSEAW	Marshall Brook	ACMRSL
The Tarn	ACTARN	Otter Creek	ACOTRC
Upper Breakneck	ACUBRK	Sargent Brook	ACSGTB
Upper Hadlock	ACUHAD	Stanley Brook	ACSTNL
Witch Hole Pond	ACWHOL		
Lake Wood	ACWOOD		

Water quality

Measures of water quality include specific conductance, pH, water temperature, and dissolved oxygen (DO). Assessment of chemistry data aids in the interpretation of the biotic condition and ecological processes of surface water resources. Specific conductance is directly related to the level of dissolved ions in the water, and can be an indicator of pollutants in the water. Most New England states indicate that a pH between 6.5 and 8.5 meets state water quality standards. The documented distribution of pH in Maine lakes by the Maine Volunteer Lake Monitoring Program (VLMP) and the Maine Department of Environmental Protection (MDEP) indicates that the pH of most Maine lakes ranged from 6.0 and 7.0 (Williams, 2004). Dissolved oxygen is a critical indicator of water quality because aquatic life generally needs DO concentrations at or above 5 mg/L to thrive. No quantitative criteria are given by the State of Maine for AA waters (the legislated classification of all Acadia National Park surface waters), but the DO content of Class A waters (the next lowest classification) shall be not less than 7 parts per million or 75 percent of saturation, whichever is higher (Maine State Government, 1985).

Specific conductance, shown in Figure 6, is within the expected range for Acadia's low ionic strength waters. The higher values in Seawall Pond (ACSEAW) and Bear Brook Pond (ACBRBK) reflect the influence of marine aerosols on these coastal sites. The three stream sites (ACBRWN, ACMRSL, ACSTNL) with higher conductance could be reflecting anthropogenic inputs, since all are located in more developed areas with histories of water quality issues. Lake and stream mean annual pH values (Figure 7) are mostly circumneutral, with the lower pH sites being likely being impacted by organic acids from associated wetlands.

Annual mean water temperatures (Figure 8) appear to be fairly consistent throughout the reporting period, with variation likely due to changing air temperature and solar radiation levels. Without exception, all of the monitored sites are well oxygenated (Figure 9), and temperatures vary in accordance with stream sources and seasonal weather conditions. Aunt Bettys Pond inlet (ACABIN) and Heath Brook (ACHTHB) DO means were slightly below the state DO standard in 2008. However, these streams, like most of the water bodies at the lower end of the DO distribution, were fed from or associated with bog/wetland systems and oxygen concentrations are in keeping with expected values for similar systems.

Water quality appears to be stable at all the monitored sites, meeting state and EPA water quality standards. It is within the limited historical range of variability for Acadia National Park waters. As more data are collected, the ability to detect changes outside this natural range of variability will increase.

Mean Annual Lake Specific Conductance (ACAD, 2006-2009)

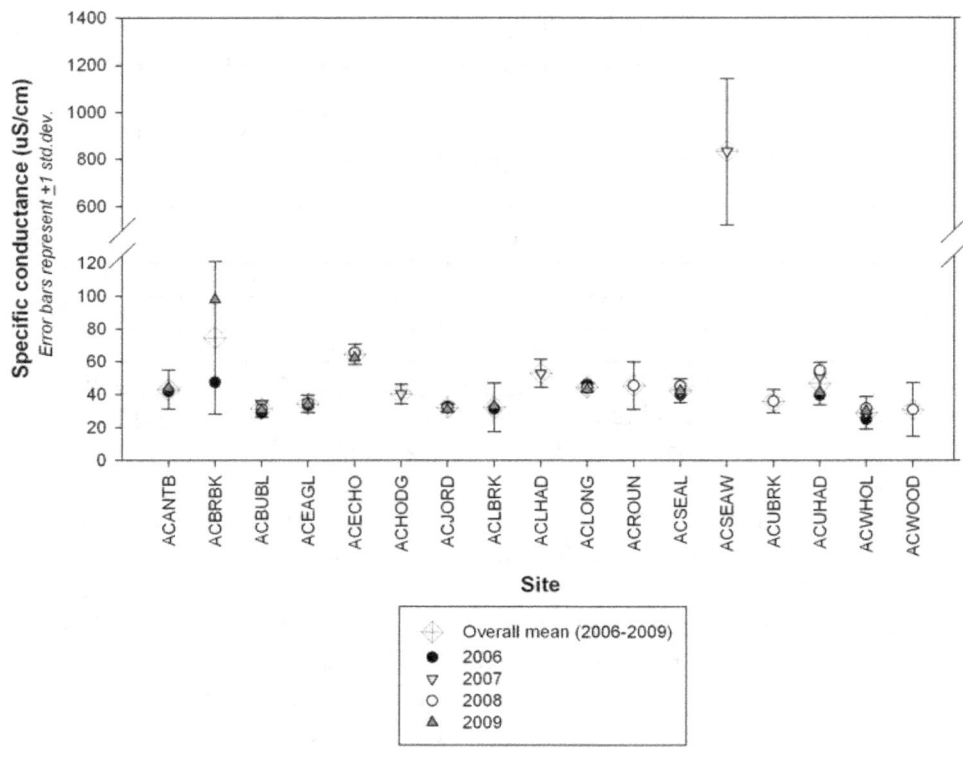

Mean Annual Stream Specific Conductance (ACAD, 2006-2009)

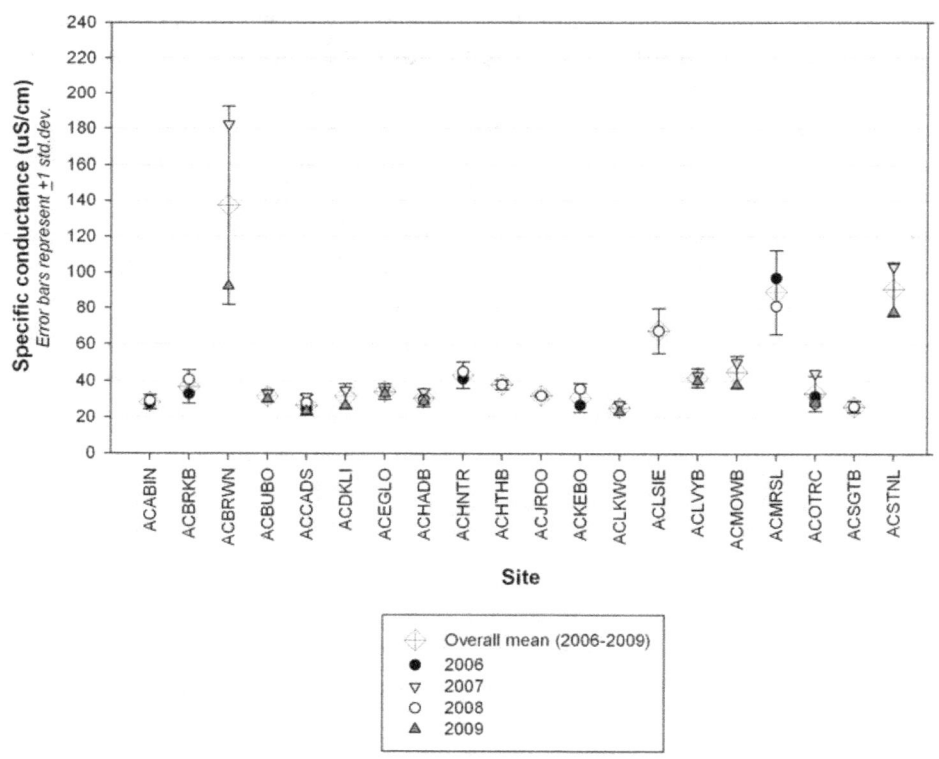

Figure 6. Specific conductance of lakes and streams.

Mean Annual Lake pH (ACAD, 2006-2009)

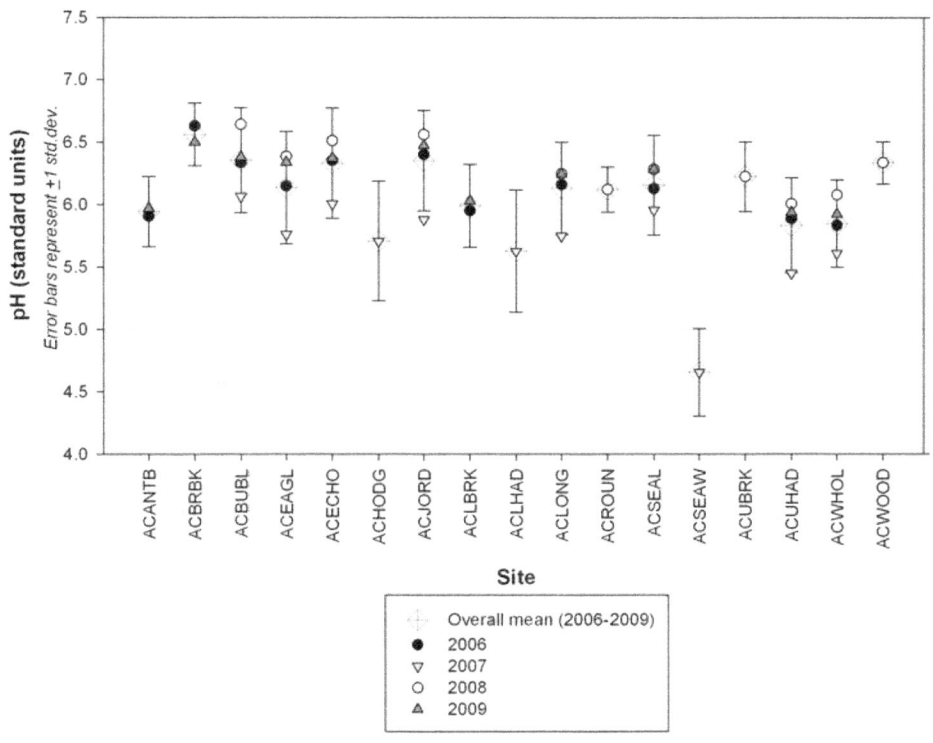

Mean Annual Stream pH (ACAD, 2006-2009)

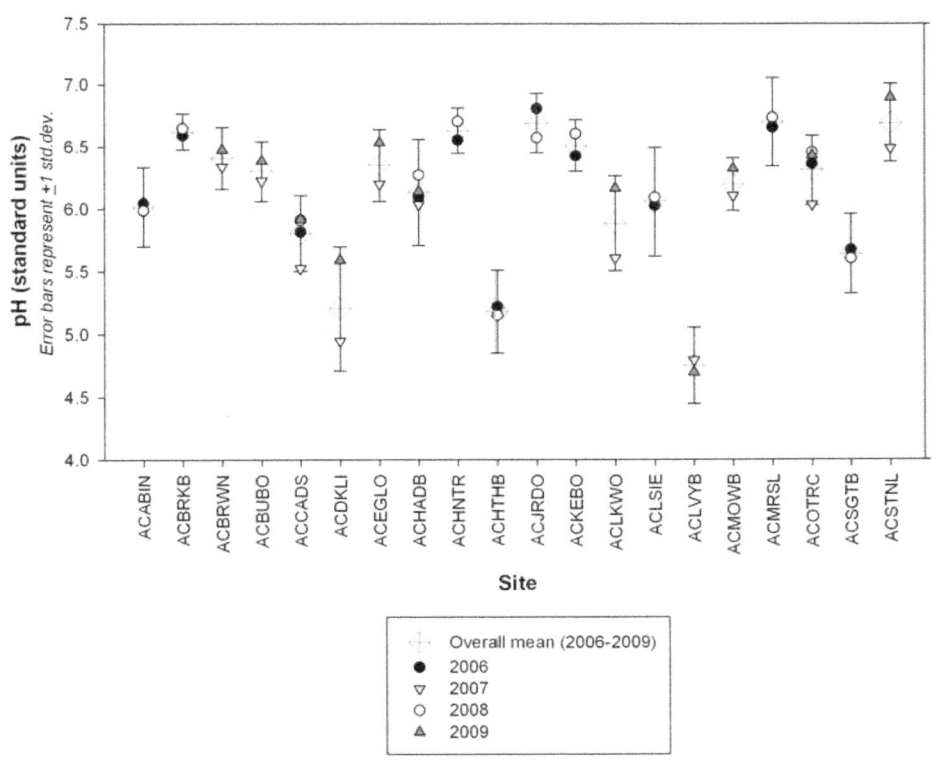

Figure 7. pH of lakes and streams.

Mean Annual LakeTemperature (ACAD, 2006-2009)

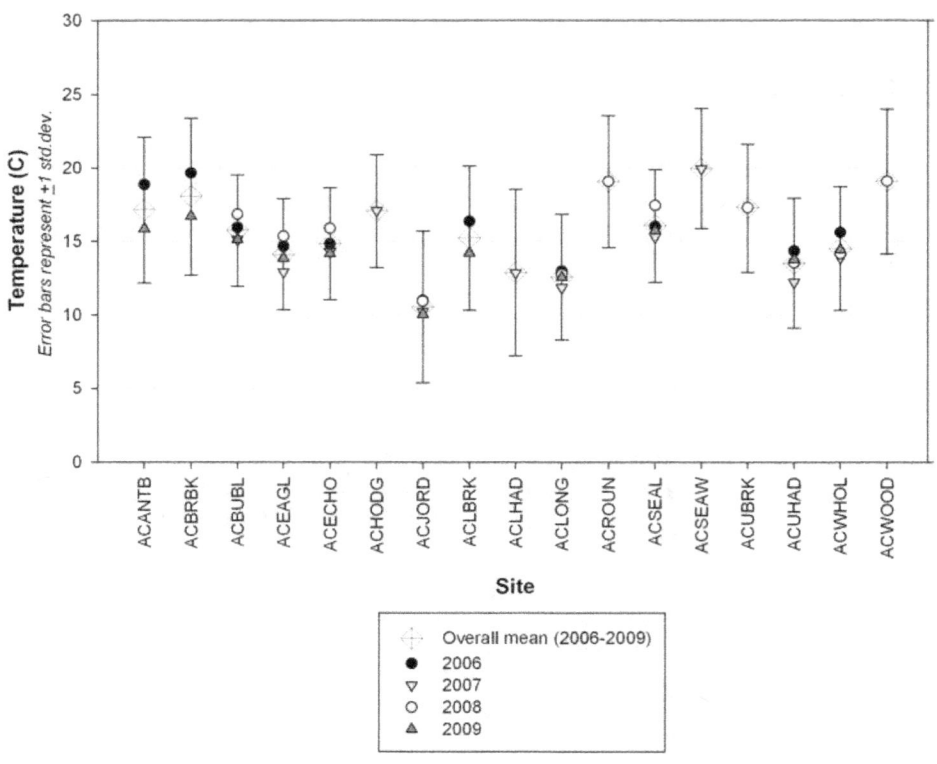

Mean Annual StreamTemperature (ACAD, 2006-2009)

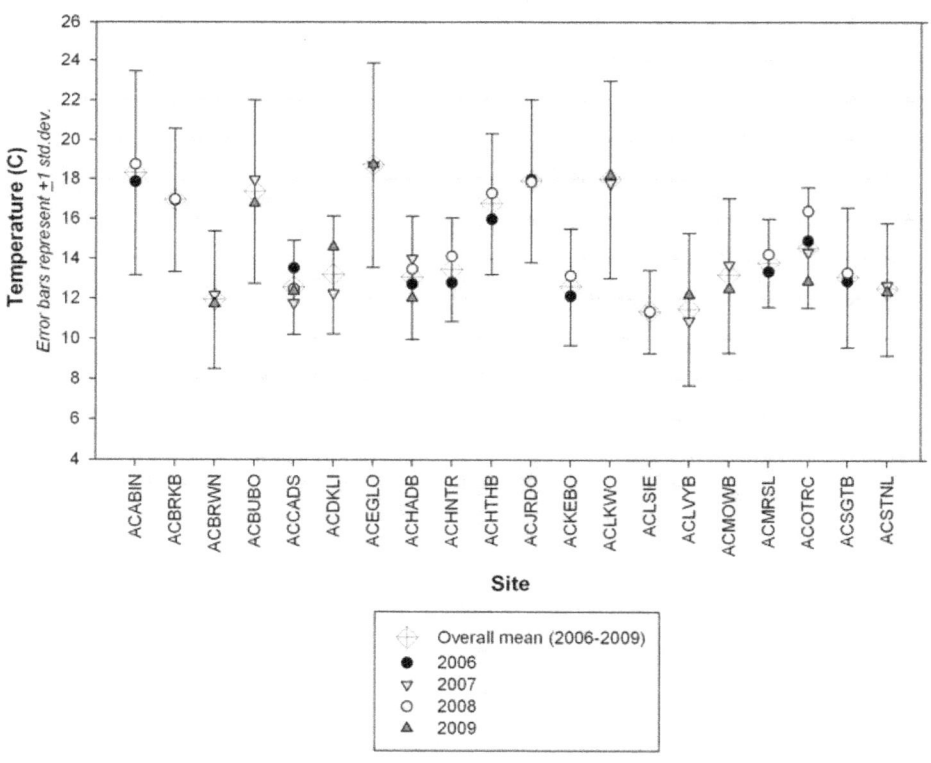

Figure 8. Temperature of lakes and streams.

Mean Annual Lake Dissolved Oxygen (ACAD, 2006-2009)

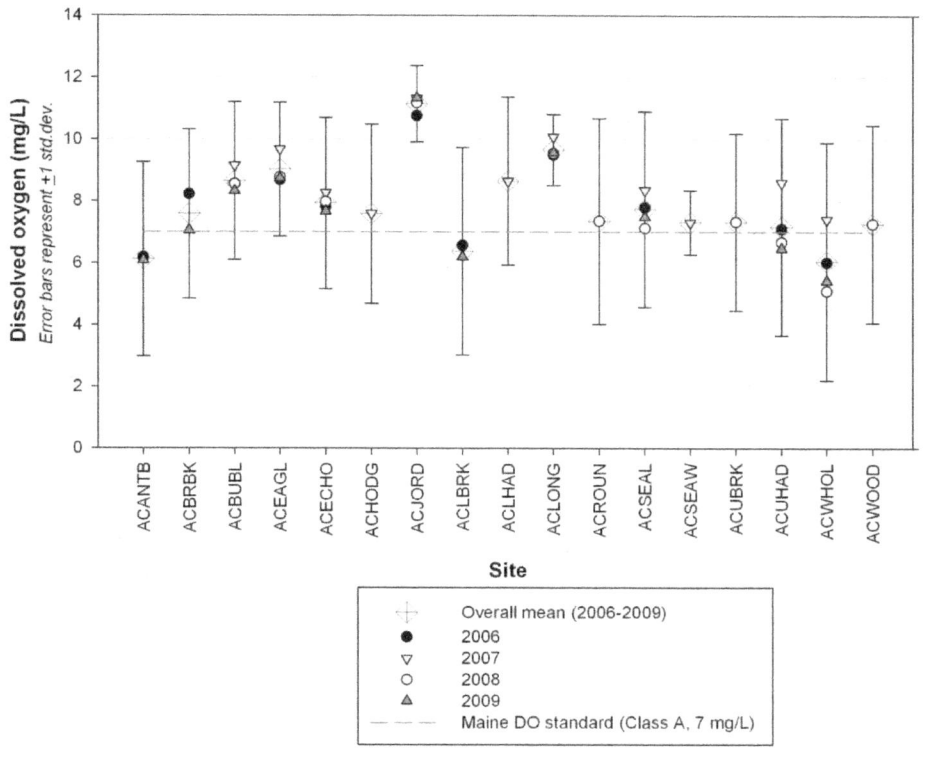

Mean Annual Stream Dissolved Oxygen (ACAD, 2006-2009)

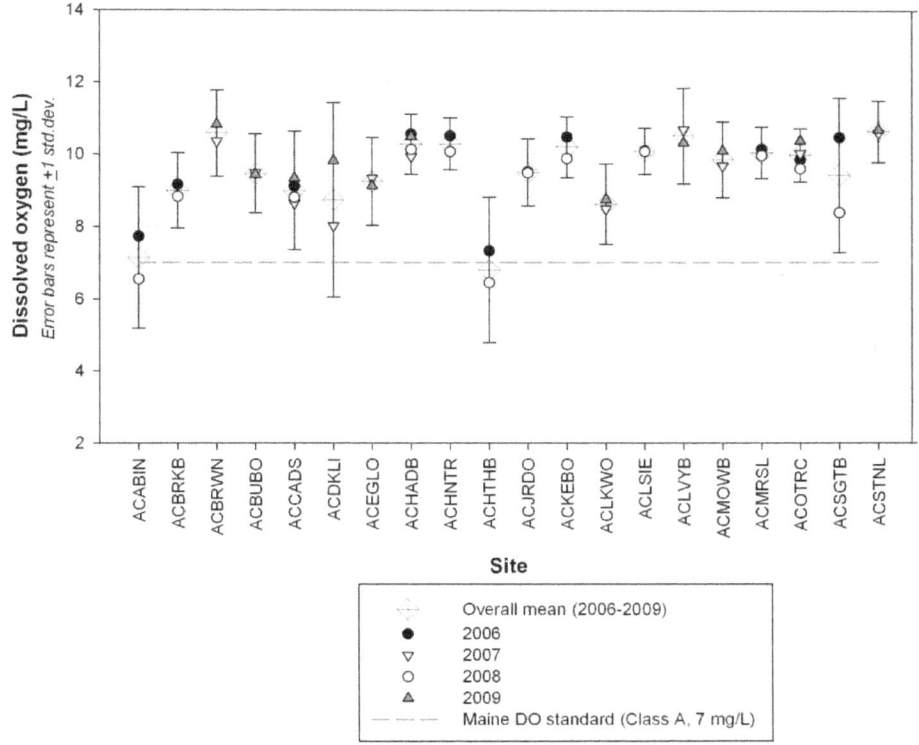

Figure 9. Dissolved oxygen of lakes and streams.

11

Nutrient Enrichment

Nutrient enrichment and the acceleration of eutrophication have been identified in most NETN parks as one of the stressors of greatest concern. Algal biomass (assessed through chlorophyll *a* samples), several forms of total and dissolved phosphorus and nitrogen, and transparency (water clarity, measured with a Secchi disk) are measured to give managers information regarding the trophic status and productivity of freshwater systems.

Transparency measurements provide simple and affordable assessments of lake productivity. Variation in precipitation is one of the major factors contributing to annual shifts in lake transparency. Often during drier conditions lakes will become clearer due to less runoff of nutrient and soil inputs. In contrast, decreased Secchi readings can often be attributed to high levels of spring and fall precipitation, and cumulative effects of high rainfall years. The driest year (2007) produced the expected increase in transparency in most lakes during the reporting period (Figure 10).

Although trophic levels of the monitored lakes range from oligotrophic (minimally productive) to eutrophic (highly productive), and a similar variety of stream types are sampled, nutrient levels are generally low. Results of water chemistry samples analyzed at the UMO labs from 2006 to 2009 indicate that values for most water quality parameters are within their historical range (when known) and do not exceed thresholds indicating that they are outside the range of natural variability.

In the lakes, seasonal (June/August) values for total phosphorus (Figure 11), total nitrogen (Figure 12) and chlorophyll *a* (Figure 13) show expected patterns similar to monitoring results of previous years. Total phosphorus (TP) and total nitrogen (TN) are generally higher in the early summer compared to late, likely due to spring runoff from snowmelt and rainfall. Chlorophyll *a* is higher in the late summer, as this is the prime growing time for phytoplankton and algae. The smaller, shallower, warmer lakes generally have higher nutrient concentrations and Seawall Pond, a shallow pond in close proximity to the ocean, is the clear outlier showing all nutrient values two to three times higher than any other lake.

Total phosphorus concentrations in the lakes range from 1.2 µg/L in Jordan Pond to 51 µg/L in Seawall Pond. Total dissolved phosphorus and orthophosphate results are proportionately lower, but followed similar trends. TN is generally below 0.5 mg/L at most sites, with Seawall Pond hitting 2.29 mg/L in August 2007. Total dissolved nitrogen ranges from 0.10 to 0.34 mg/L (excepting 2 high Seawall values). Lake concentrations of other nitrogen analytes (nitrate, nitrite, ammonia) are extremely low, with many results below laboratory reporting limits. Most lakes have chlorophyll *a* values below 4 µg/L.

Nutrient parameters for streams are in similar ranges as those for lakes. Lurvey Brook, Marshall Brook, and Heath Brook, all draining from wetlands on the west side of Mount Desert Island, have the highest TP and TN levels. The very high total phosphorus value (38 µg/L) for the Lurvey Brook sample collected in August 2007 may be a result of sample contamination. Because of the limited amount of historical water quality information available for many of the stream sites and the short current monitoring history, it will be several years before any trend analysis will be possible.

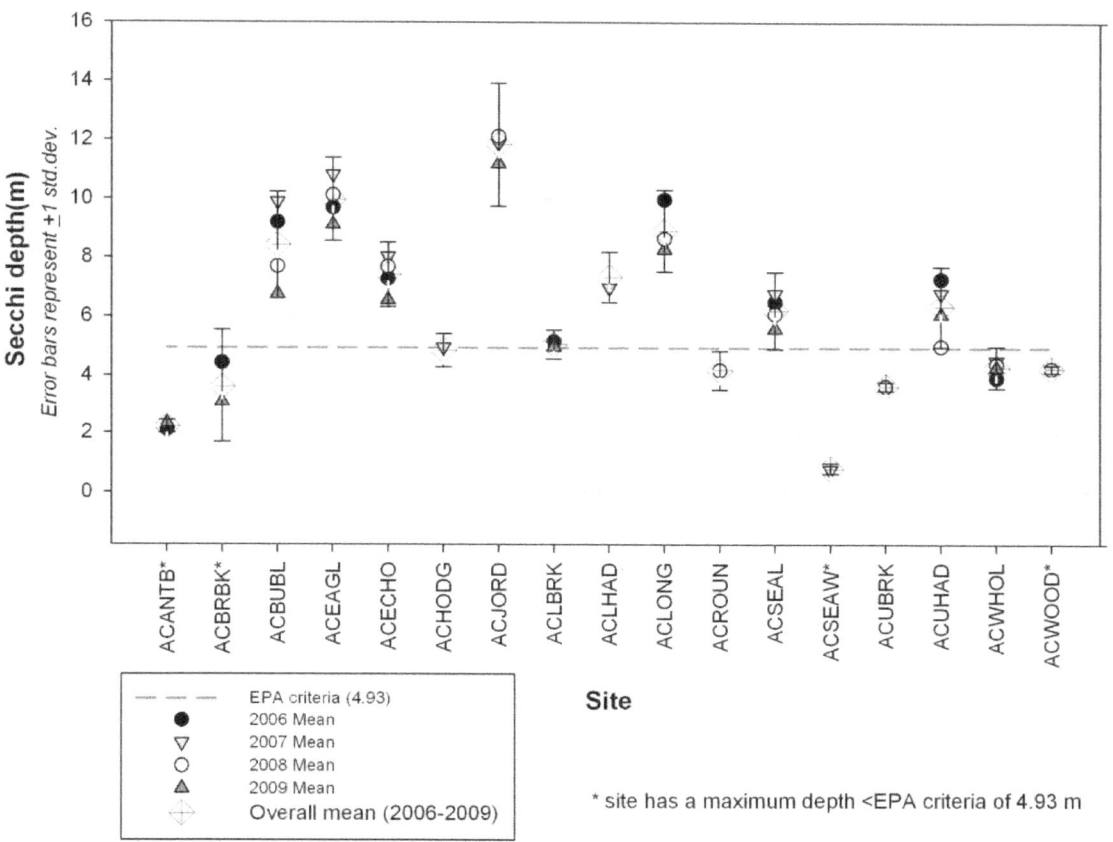

Figure 10. Lake transparency.

Total Phosphorus: ACAD Lakes (2006-2009)

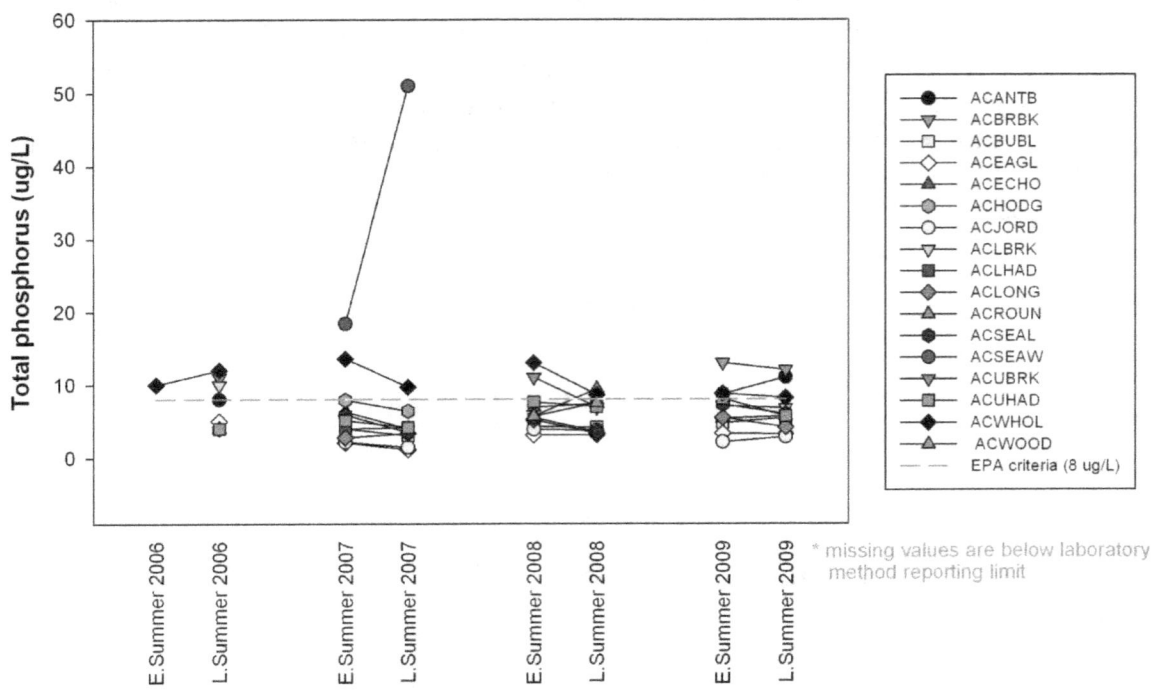

Total Phosphorus: ACAD Streams (2006-2009)

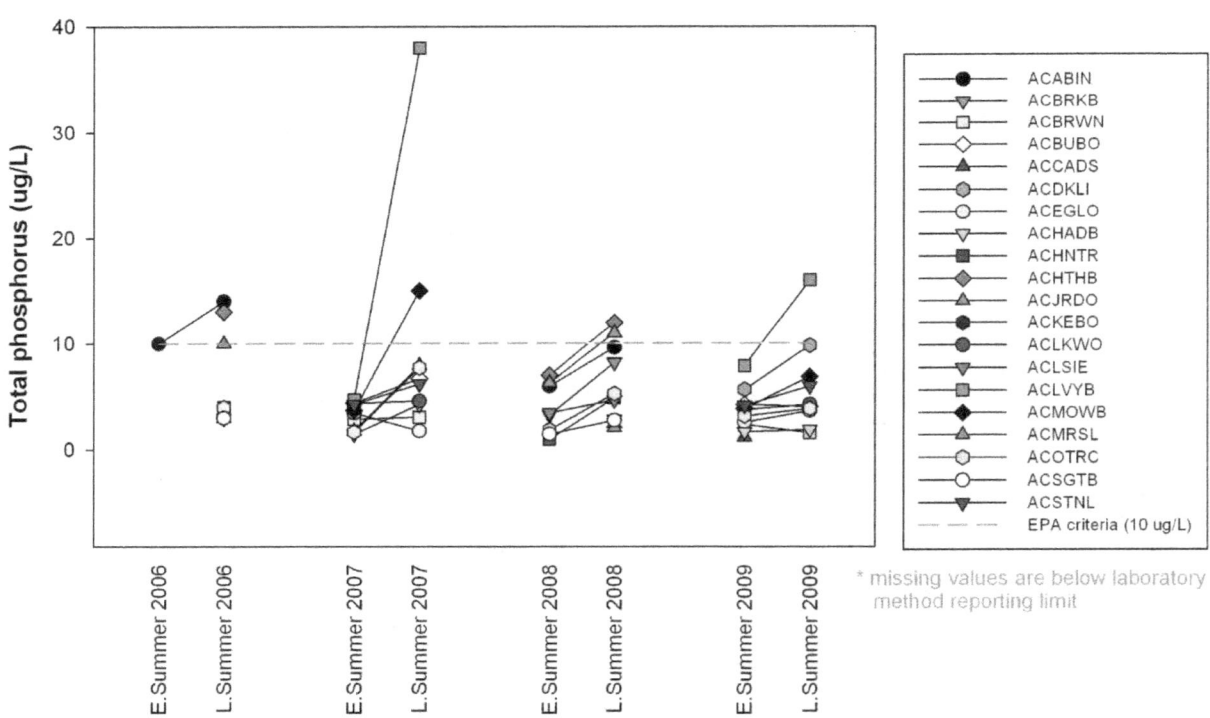

Figure 11. Total phosphorus in lakes and streams

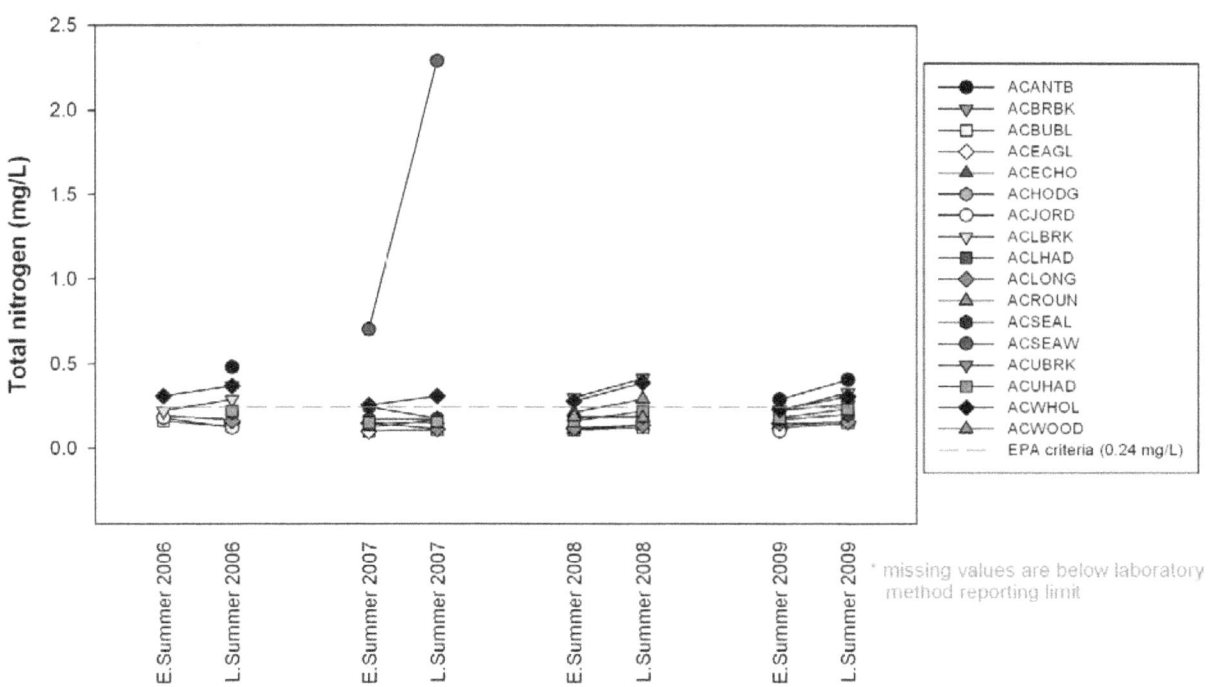

Total Nitrogen: ACAD Lakes (2006-2009)

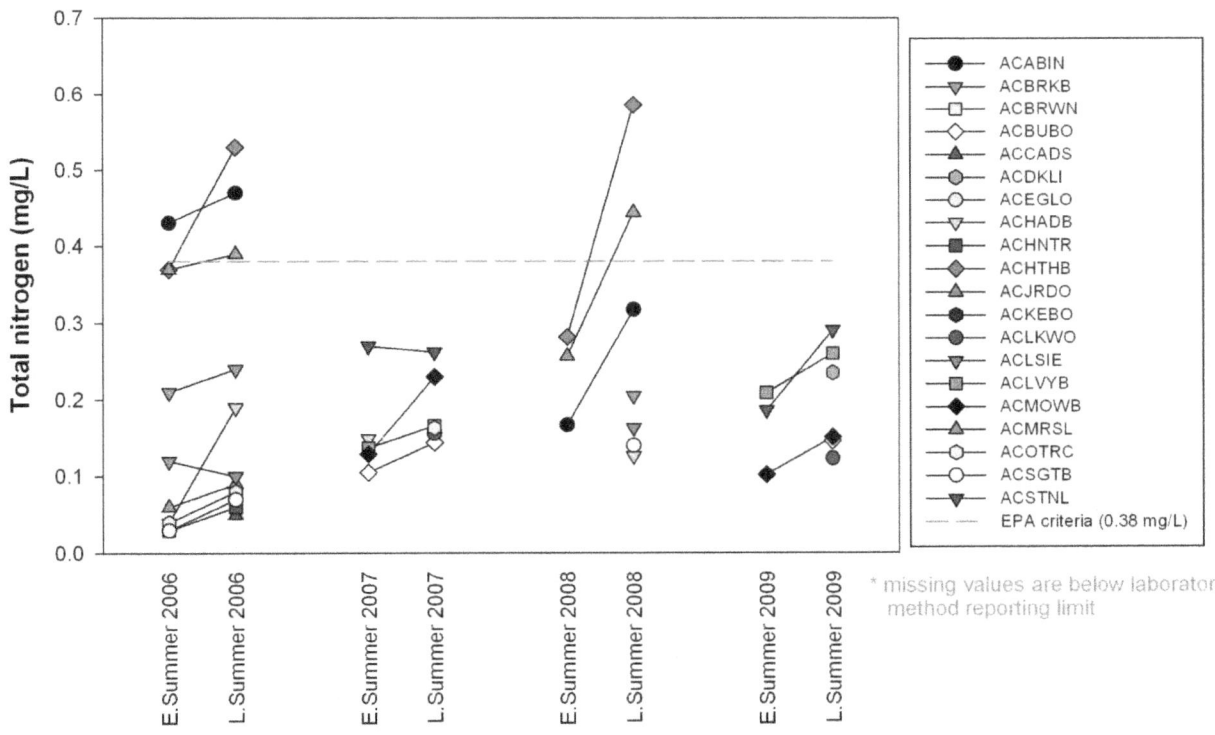

Total Nitrogen: ACAD Streams (2006-2009)

Figure 12. Total nitrogen in lakes and streams.

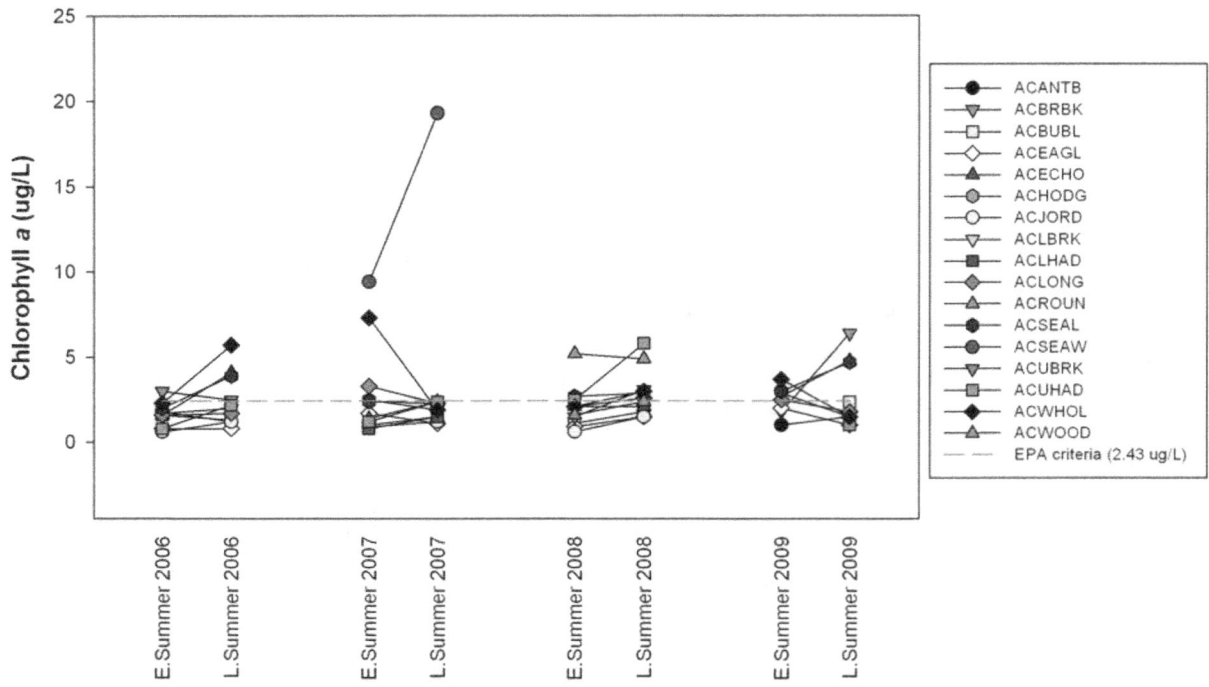

Figure 13. Chlorophyll *a* in lakes.

Water Quantity

Weekly water level (stage) measurements from up to 17 lakes are averaged and overlaid on weekly total precipitation plots to document changes over the course of the monitoring seasons. Mean weekly changes in 2006 and 2007 (Figure 14) are less variable in the summer months than those in 2008 and 2009 (Figure 15). As depicted in Figure 16, some lakes and ponds (often those altered by beaver populations) are "flashier" than others. Detailed analysis of watershed characteristics may further explain the variability between sites.

The USGS stream gage at Otter Creek provides a continuous discharge record that can be used as an index for the other monitored streams on Mount Desert Island (Figure 17). Plots of data from the Global water level loggers at Cadillac and Hadlock Brooks show a very strong similarity to the Otter Creek data, though discharge levels are far lower in the former sites, which are near the top of their watersheds (Figure 18).

Monthly stream discharge measurements (Figure 19), taken with a current meter and wading rod, can be used to calculate loading of nutrient chemical constituents, and also provide a record of seasonal variations in stream flow. Stream stage measurements, taken by measuring to the water surface from a fixed datum point, can be paired with discharge values, and over time a stage/discharge relationship can be calculated. Once this relationship is established, monitors can interpolate the stream discharge from the stage measurement alone.

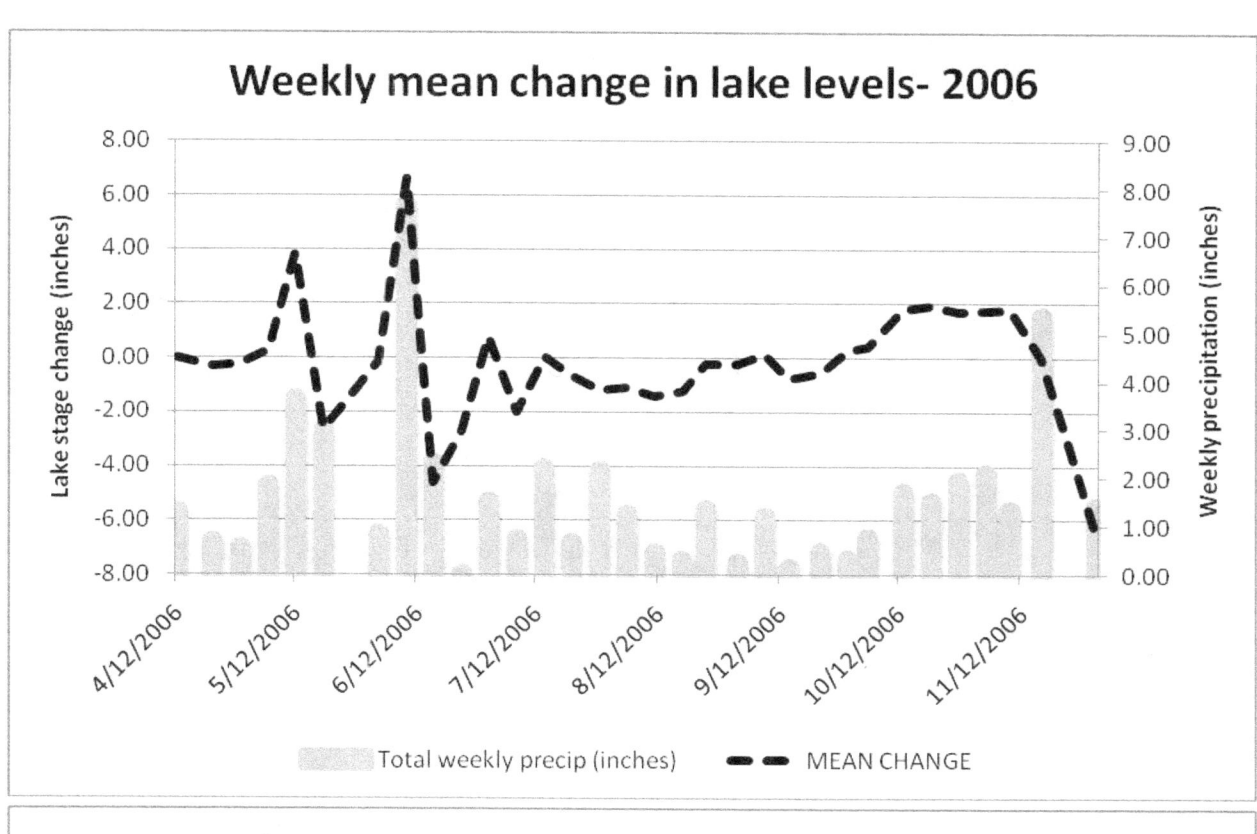

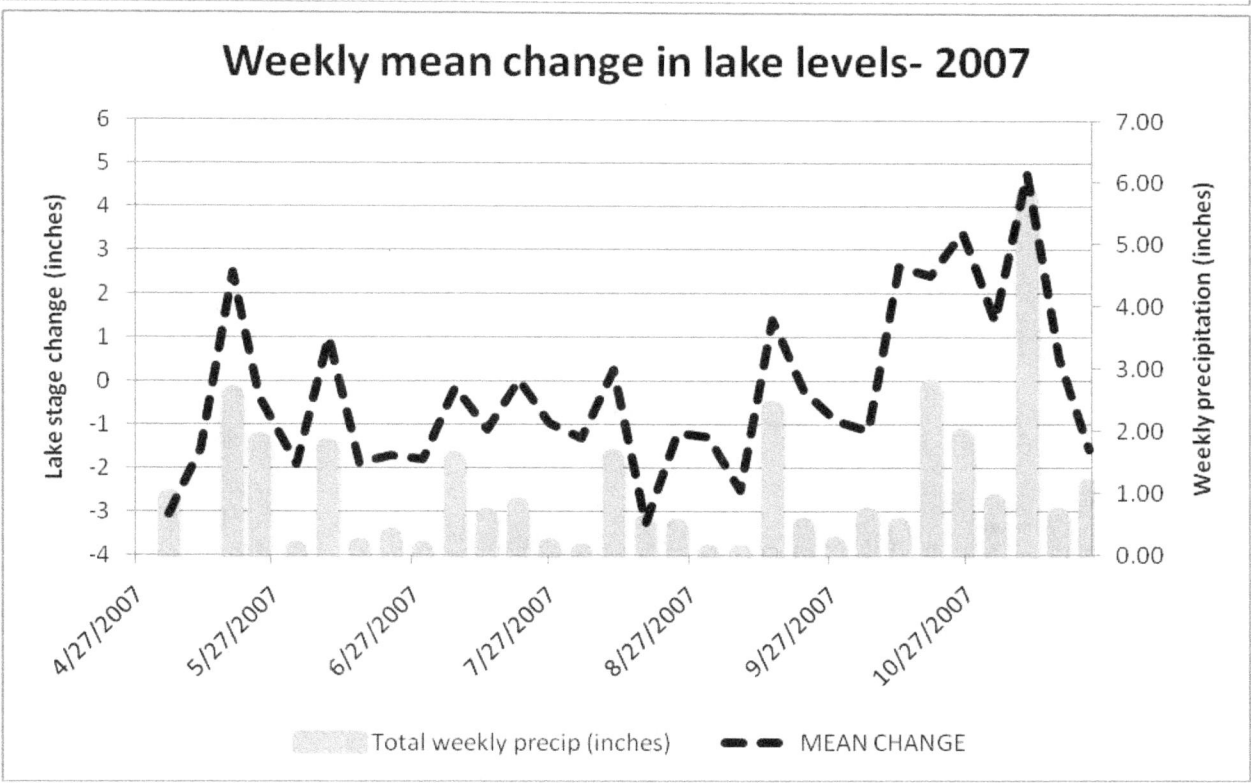

Figure 14. Mean weekly lake levels in 2006 and 2007.

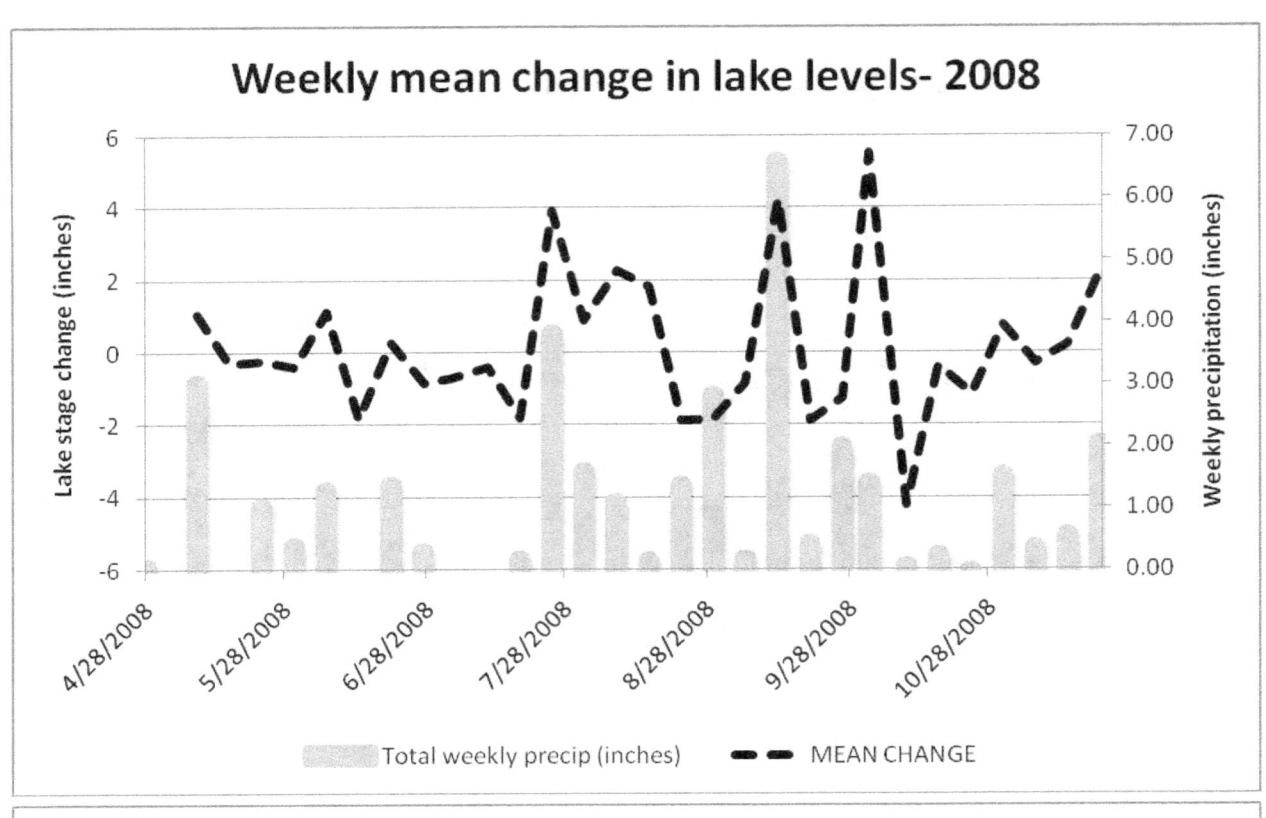

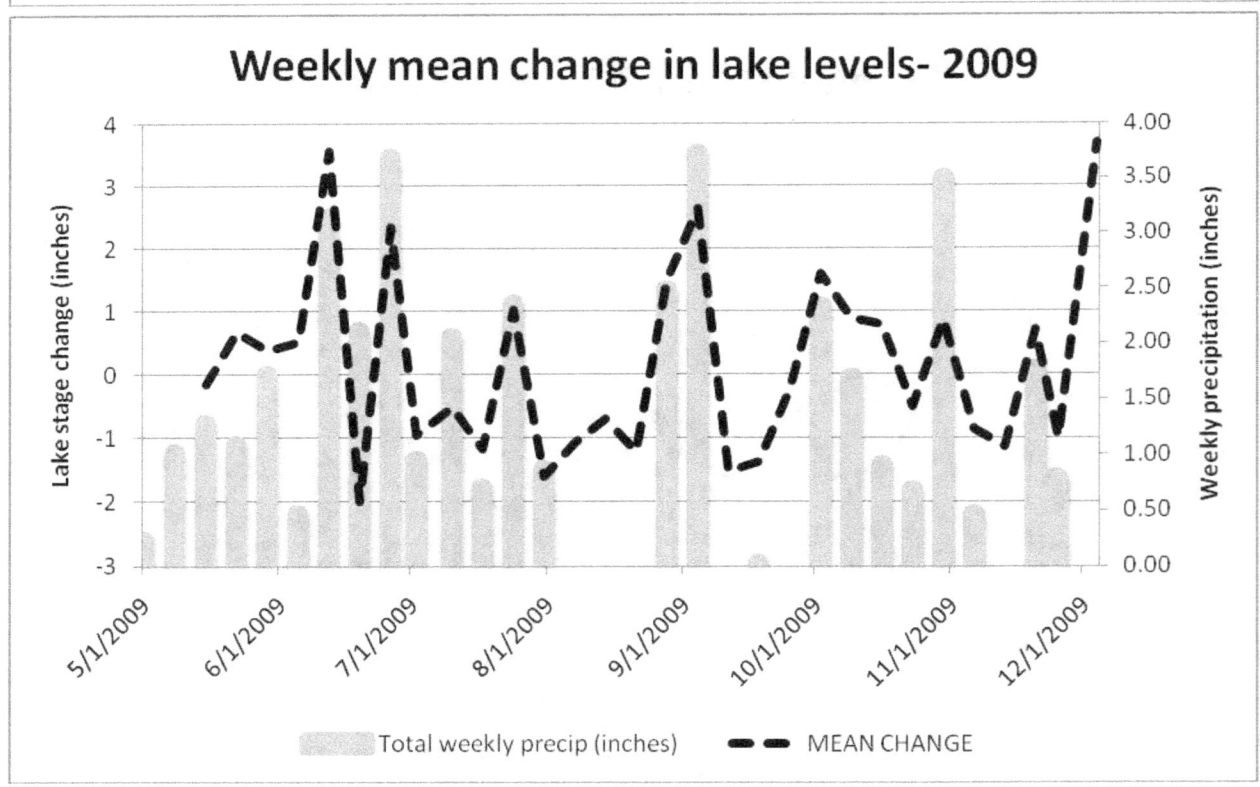

Figure 15. Mean weekly lake levels in 2008 and 2009.

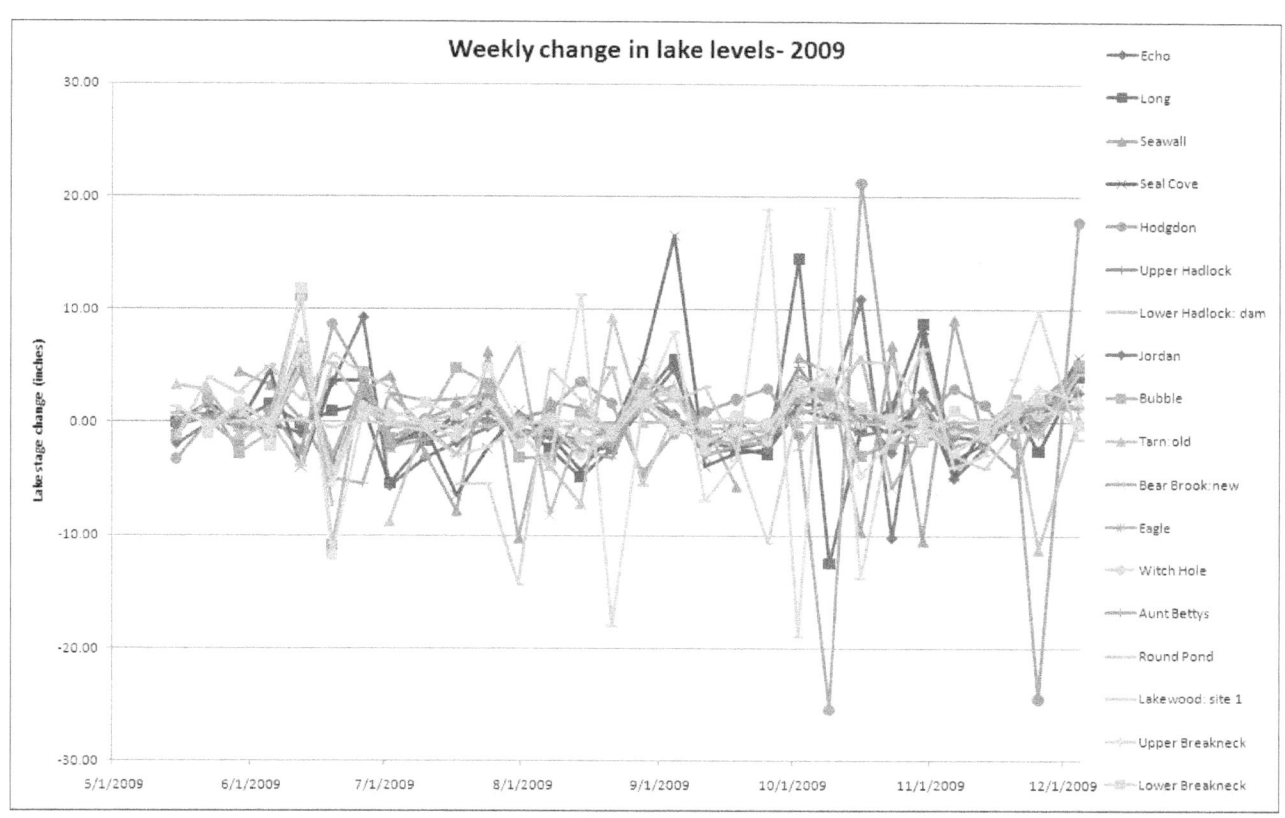

Figure 16. Weekly lake levels for all lakes in 2009 (note complexity of variation between sites).

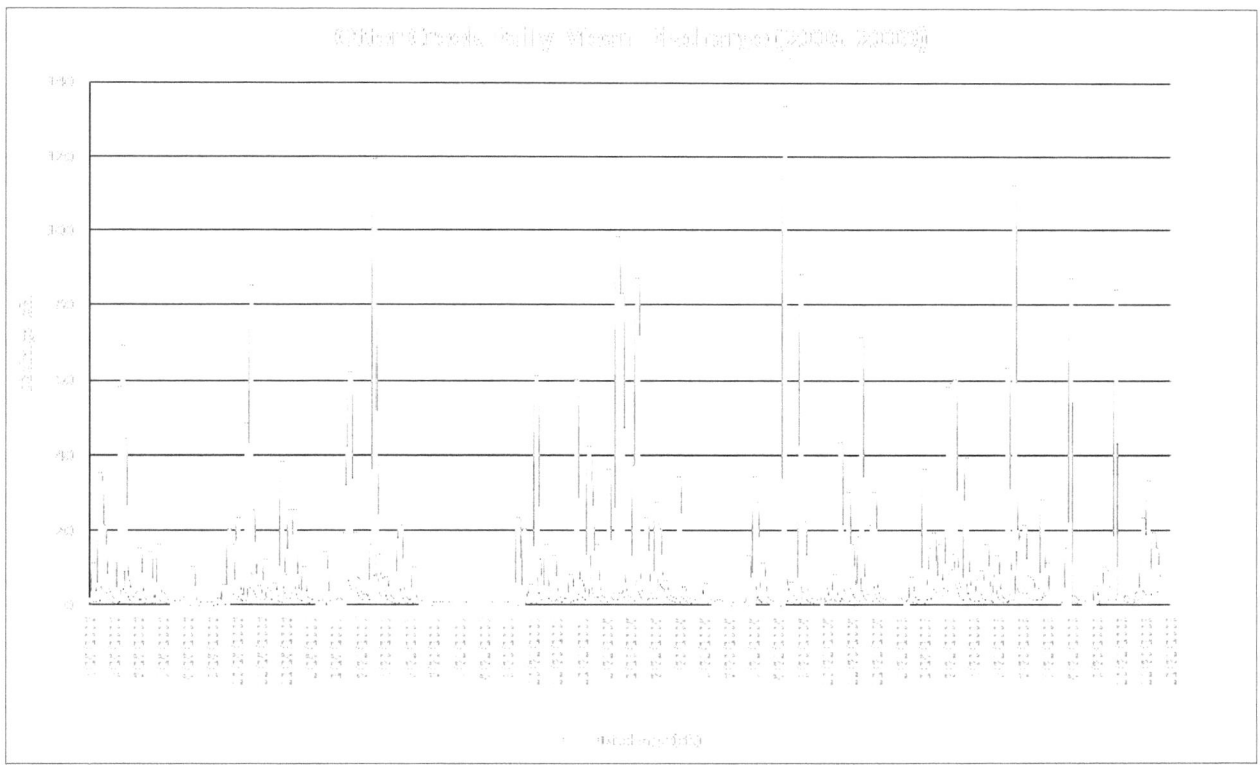

Figure 17. Discharge from the primary continuous record site at Otter Creek (2006-2009).

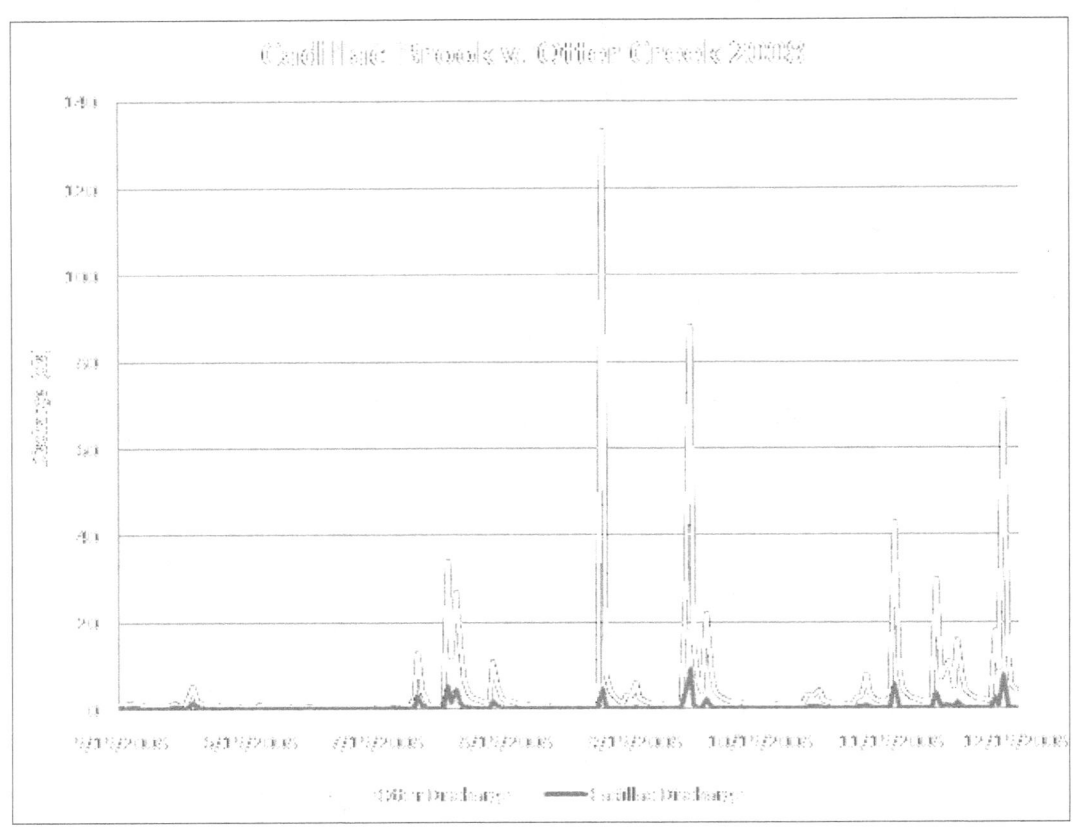

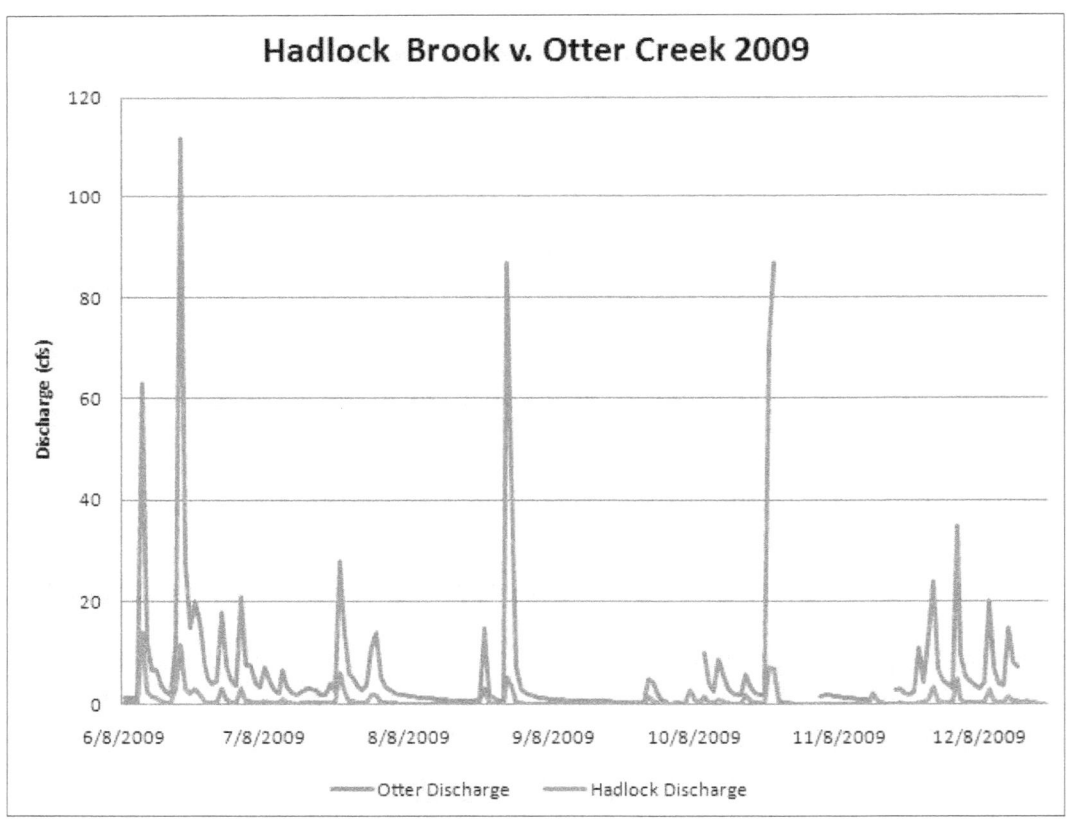

Figure 18. Discharge data from secondary continuous record sites.

Invasive Aquatic Plants

Methods for invasive aquatic plant monitoring are adapted from the Maine Center for Invasive Aquatic Plants (MCIAP), a division of the Volunteer Lake Monitoring Program (VLMP). Detailed survey instructions can be found in the NETN protocol (Lombard et al. 2006). Acadia National Park staff attend yearly Invasive Plant Patrol (IPP) trainings led by the MCIAP. Since non-native, invasive plants have recently been found in over 20 Maine lakes, it has become crucial to closely monitor the status of park waters. The early detection of an infestation can make eradication or control more feasible, and it can lead to efforts that reduce the spread of the plant to neighboring waterbodies. Designating the early detection of these plants as a NETN vital sign and the ongoing partnership with state and local monitoring and eradication efforts are highly effective prevention strategies. Table 4 provides a list of lakes monitored for invasive plants during the 2006 through 2009 seasons.

Table 4. Acadia NP lakes monitored for invasive aquatic plants

2006	2007	2008	2009
Eagle Lake	Eagle Lake	Eagle Lake	Eagle Lake
Echo Lake	Echo Lake	Echo Lake	Echo Lake
		Hodgdon Pond	Hodgdon Pond
Jordan Pond	Jordan Pond	Jordan Pond	Jordan Pond
Long Pond	Long Pond	Long Pond	Long Pond
Lower Hadlock	Lower Hadlock	Lower Hadlock	Lower Hadlock
	Seal Cove Pond	Seal Cove Pond	Seal Cove Pond
Upper Hadlock	Upper Hadlock	Upper Hadlock	Upper Hadlock

The primary targets of the invasive plant surveys are the 11 plants currently listed by the MCIAP as imminent threats to Maine waters. These are:

European Frogbit (*Hydrocharis morsus-ranae*)

Water Chestnut (*Trapa natans*)

Yellow Floating Heart (*Nymphoides peltata*)

Eurasian Water Milfoil (*Myriophyllum spicatum*)

Variable Water Milfoil (*Myriophyllum heterophyllum*)

Parrot Feather (*Myriophyllum aquaticum*)

Fanwort (*Cabomba caroliniana*)

Hydrilla (*Hydrilla verticillata*)

Brazilian Elodea (*Egeria densa*)

European Naiad (*Najas minor*)

Curly-Leaved Pondweed (*Potamogeton crispus*)

Monitoring did not detect these invasive aquatic plants in any of Acadia's surveyed ponds.

Summary

The adoption of NETN lake and stream monitoring protocols during the 2006 season bolsters the ability to detect changes in the quality and quantity of Acadia NP surface waters, while retaining data comparability with the park's ongoing acidification effects monitoring, stream macroinvertebrate monitoring, invasive aquatic plant surveys, and historic water quality records dating back to the early 1980s. This report does not attempt to determine long-term trends for specific water chemistry parameters, since not all sites have a sufficient data history to enable trend detection. This is especially the case with stream sites, most of which were not monitored regularly by park staff before the inception of the NETN program.

It is clear that changes in water quantity, and their effects on water quality, must be evaluated in concert with the apparently increased variation in annual and seasonal environmental/climatic patterns experienced in recent years. Lake levels and stream flows vary in accordance with seasonal precipitation trends. Dissolved oxygen levels are within the expected ranges (Williams 2004) for the trophic type of each water body. Results of summer (May-June/August) nutrient sampling show that phosphorus, nitrogen and chlorophyll *a* concentrations from 2006 to 2009 are relatively low, and are generally within the historical range of variability (Seger, et al. 2005) for Acadia NP waters.

In summary, 4 years of monitoring under the NETN protocol have provided critical information on the chemical and physical status of Acadia National Park lakes and streams. Refinements of the monitoring protocol and enhanced QA/QC procedures have improved the data quality with each subsequent year, allowing a better understanding of the seasonal and temporal variability of individual constituents within each water body. As more data are collected, the ability to detect changes outside this natural range of variability will increase, which in turn will more clearly indicate the status of the vital signs of water chemistry, nutrient enrichment, water quantity, and the detection of invasive plant species.

Literature Cited

Lombard, P., W. Gawley, ,J. Caldwell, 2006, Freshwater Vital-Signs Monitoring Plan for National Parks in the Northeast Temperate Network (NETN) PHASE III: Water-Quality Monitoring Protocols in Lakes, Ponds and Streams : USGS, Augusta, ME, 222 p.

Maine State Government, 1985, Maine statutes, Title 38, Section 464(4)(F)) accessed on September 12, 2005 at *http://janus.state.me.us/legis/statutes/38/title38sec464.html*.

Seger, E.M., W.G. Gawley, and R.M. Breen. 2005. Acadia National Park Lake monitoring report 2002 to 2005: Acadia National Park Natural Resource Report 05-06.

Williams, S., 2004, Maine volunteer lake monitoring annual report, Volunteer lake monitoring program, accessed on September 12, 2005 at: *http://mainevolunteerlakemonitors.org/index2.htm*.

U.S. Environmental Protection Agency, 2002, Ecoregional nutrient criteria: U.S. Environmental Protection Agency Fact Sheet USEPA-822-F-02-008, October 2002.